Abram believed th LORD, and he cou it to him as righteousness. Genesis 15:6

Lead me, O LORD, in your righteousness; make your way straight before me.
Psalm 5:8

He judges the world with righteousness; he judges the peoples with uprightness. Psalm 9:8

The heavens declare his righteousness, for God himself is judge! Psalm 50:6

There is none righteous, no not one.

Romans 3:10

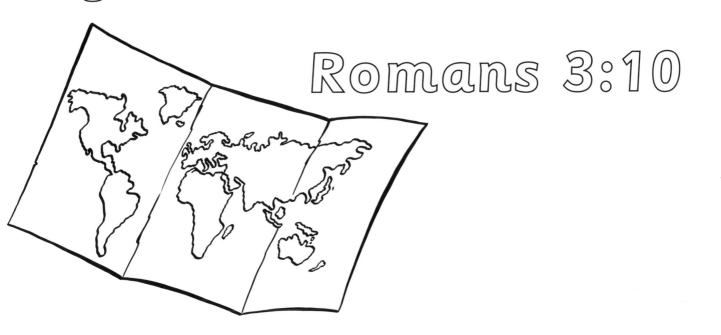

Righteousness exalts
a nation, but sin is a
reproach to any people.

Proverbs 14:34

Those who turn many to righteousness shall shine like the stars forever and ever. Daniel 12:3

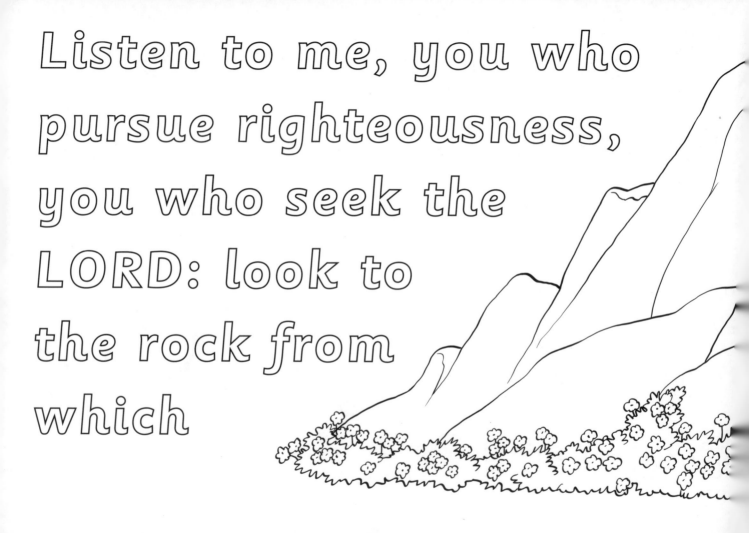

Listen to me, you who pursue righteousness, you who seek the LORD: look to the rock from which

you were hewn, and
to the quarry from
which you
were dug.
Isaiah 51:1

Let justice roll
down like
waters,
and
righteousness like an
ever-flowing stream.
Amos 5:24

When he comes, he will convict the world concerning sin and righteousness and judgment. John 16:8

The kingdom of God is not a matter of eating and drinking but of

righteousness and peace and joy in the Holy Spirit. Romans 14: 17

For our sake he made him to be sin who knew no sin, so that in him we

might become the

righteousness of God.

2 Corinthians 5:21

What is righteousness? It is when someone is right and perfect. God is perfect. He is holy. He is righteous. All he does and says and is – is right. People aren't righteous. We are sinners. The wrong things we do, think and say displease God. But God wants us to be righteous so that we can be saved from sin and hell. God sent Jesus to die on the cross so that his righteousness could be given freely to those who trust in him. The only way to be made righteous is to believe in the Lord Jesus Christ.

When you trust that Jesus' death can save you from sin and guilt then God gives you Christ's righteousness. It is just as though you are righteous and always have been. Jesus' righteousness covers your sinfulness.